The Lost
Churches and Chapels
of Sussex

Alex Vincent

S. B. Publications

First published in 2005 by S. B. Publications
Tel: 01323 893498
Email: sbpublications@tiscali.co.uk

ISBN 1-85770-303-0

Front cover pictures: Lullington, Binderton, Ore, Church Norton
Back cover: Winchelsea

Designed and Typeset by EH Graphics (01273) 515527
Printed by Ethos Productions Ltd.

Introduction

Throughout the country there are a vast number of lost churches and chapels either standing in ruins, no visible remains above ground, or redundant. In the case of the former, some may have several walls remaining, only a few stones, just foundations, or could be complete, but roofless. In the case of no visible remains above ground, an earthen mound or earthworks may mark their sites and in some cases only the graveyard remains. Some sites have been built over and a plaque sometimes marks them. In redundant churches, they are either not in use or have only a few services each year.

The loss of churches and chapels can be for several reasons and one is neglect where the parishioners were too poor to repair them. Another is the desertion of the village which it once served. In most lost villages the church still stands today and is in use, serving other nearby settlements, which either lost their church or never possessed one. Some churches came out of use at the Dissolution of the Monastries and French attacks, war etc. are other reasons why they became lost. Some ruined churches were rebuilt, incorporating the remains of the original into the new, such as at Durrington and Aldrington in Sussex.

A number of churches and chapels have been lost to the sea by coastal erosion and the most famous case is at Dunwich in Suffolk. This was once a city, which had a fair number of churches and chapels now lost beneath the waves between the 12th and 20th centuries. The east coast of Britain suffered much coastal erosion over the centuries. Rocks visible at low tides are said to be the remains of a church, but any building would have crumbled away in the sea. In most cases of churches out at sea, there is a legend that the bells can still be heard chiming in the tower at certain times of the year.

Lost churches and chapels come into three categories, which are 1. just its site where there are no visible remains, 2. standing in ruins, and 3. still a complete church, but in use as some other function or derelict. In the case of the latter, only its original use is lost and could well become a place of worship again in the future. Some churches and chapels are only partly lost, where only the chancel for example is in use, but the nave is either in ruins or nothing remaining above ground such as at Lullington in Sussex.

The sites of lost churches and chapels (ruins, no visible remains etc.) are mainly owned by someone such as the National Trust, English Heritage, or in private ownership. Permission must be sought to visit those on private land, but some can be seen from nearby footpaths. Others are just overgrown ruins by a farm, in a field or woodland, but in most cases a footpath passes close by. Some ruins can be dangerous (particularly those which are overgrown) and care must be taken to visit them. If in doubt then it is best not to go into them and only view them from the nearby footpath or road. This also applies to churches lost beneath the waves, where the sea can be a dangerous place, and cliff edges which can be very treacherous, so care must be taken at low tides and at the top and bottom of cliffs.

This book gives details of the lost churches and chapels in Sussex, and all photographs were taken by the author. Of places which had more than one church in Medieval times, which are mentioned under the one heading, then the photograph is of the title such as Chichester All Saints in the Pallant. Where the title does not mention any particular church like Hastings parishes churches, then the accompanying photograph will be mentioned in the text such as "pictured here". This will also apply to where the site of the lost church or chapel is uncertain if there is more than one possible site for it. The lost churches and chapels in this book date from the Medieval period or earlier, unless they were rebuilt in Victorian times, but are now lost.

Acknowledgements

I wish to thank those who have helped with the preparation of this book such as various archaeological societies, libraries, record offices and friends. I also thank those who gave me permission to photograph lost churches and chapels, which are on their land and who own them.

Alex Vincent. 2005.

Contents

Angmering St Nicholas

In Medieval times the village of Angmering had two churches, which were St Margaret and St Nicholas. Only that of St Margaret exists today. In St Nicholas Garden at the back of The Lamb Inn is a pile of stones. These are the only visible remains of the old church of St Nicholas, which stood on the site since Saxon times. It was demolished in the latter part of the 16th century.

This was the parish church of East Angmering and that of St Margaret some 100 yards away was the parish church of West Angmering before the Reformation. These parishes of East and West Angmering were divided by a north to south lane, which is now Arundel Road. The latter became the parish church of Angmering when the benefices were amalgamated in 1573.

The site of St Nicholas church was excavated by the Sussex Archaeological Field Unit in 1974 and they found evidence that a church stood here in Saxon times and that it was altered in the 12th, 14th and 15th centuries. Also a couple of tombs were found. The church consisted of a nave, chancel, aisle and tower. Glazed floor tiles and glass of the 14th and 15th centuries from the church are on display in Worthing Museum.

Atherington

The church and village of Atherington west of Littlehampton was lost to the sea by coastal erosion towards the end of the 17th century. Today nothing can be seen of the church or village at low tide and it is said that the bells can be heard ringing in the tower at certain times of the year. There is very little information on Atherington church.

To the north of Atherington is Bailiffscourt, which was a grange of the great Benedictine Abbey of Seez in Normandy. All trace of the Norman building is lost except for a few stones and a 13th century chapel (pictured here). The existing building was built in 1928 in the Medieval style and is now a hotel. Other old buildings in the vicinity came from elsewhere.

The 13th century chapel is a single building with a large east window. It was in use as a store shed and is now used for blessings. In the south-east corner of the chapel is a stone with a Medieval mass dial on it. This was washed up on the shore and probably came from the submerged Atherington church. It is thought that Bailiffscourt may have been a hamlet chapel as well as a manorial one, probably after Atherington church was lost.

Balsdean

Balsdean chapel, some two miles north of Rottingdean, was built in the 12th century to serve the hamlet of that name. It consisted of a nave and chancel. In a charter of 1121 Rottingdean church is mentioned, but not Balsdean chapel. In 1579 the vicar of Rottingdean was required to hold four services a year in the chapel and not long after this it ceased to be used.

There is a view of the chapel by Lambert in c.1775 in the Burrell Collection in the British Museum. It is the oldest view of it and shows the nave with a thatched roof and parts of the ruined chancel. By 1780 it was used as a stable and the chancel had collapsed by this time. The chapel was demolished during World War II.

The chapel was excavated between 1945 and 1953 and revealed that the chancel was apsidal and the south wall of the nave was also extended. Three burials were found (two being children) and thought to be Medieval. The site of the chapel today is represented by a slight mound with a plaque marking the site of the altar.

Bargham

The site of the church of Bargham is situated in a field west of Upper Barpham Farm some four miles north of Angmering. The Church consisted of an early Saxon nave and chancel and in the late Saxon period north and south transepts were added. These transepts were given an apse as well as the chancel in the 12th century. The chancel was converted to a rectangular east end in the 13th century.

The church was demolished in about 1500 and stones from it were used in the farmhouse and barns at the adjacent farm. The site of the church was excavated in the 1950s and a number of items were found such as Horsham slab, a fragment of the font, graves and a priest's doorway on the south wall of the chancel.

On the site today is a mound, which represents the site of the former church. There is some walling and it is not part of the church foundations, but it may be the remains of the churchyard wall. The Saxon church and its village (deserted by the Black Death) were not mentioned in the Domesday Book.

Bilsham

The small chapel at Bilsham dates from the 13th century and it is a single rectangular building. It has two light windows on the north wall of c.1260 and also on the east end dating to the 14th century. The chapel ceased to be used for worship sometime before the mid-16th century. It was once used as a shed and is now a homely dwelling called "The Old Chapel".

Binderton

Binderton is mentioned in the Domesday Book as "Bertredtone" and also a church. The church had a nave, chancel and steeple in the 16th century and in 1660 Thomas Smith (who built Binderton House) got it demolished because it blocked his view. The site of the church is in the grounds of Binderton House at the junction of the A286 main road and Binderton Lane.

In c.1671 Thomas Smith's son (also Thomas) built a chapel at Binderton (pictured here) to replace the parish church, but it was never consecrated. Only one burial took place in it, which was Thomas Smith Junior in 1688. In 1839 his body and monument were removed to West Dean church.

Binderton chapel was a single chambered building and there was a round arched doorway at its west end with a window over it. There was a wooden-framed two-light window at the east wall, but no windows on the north and south walls. The chapel was used as a granary in the 18th century and it is now a roofless ruin with a plaque giving details about it.

Bognor

The original settlement of Bognor together with its chapel was lost to the sea by coastal erosion in the early part of the 17th century. There is very little information about the chapel, which was probably built in the 13th century. It was dedicated to St Bartholomew and was merged with the vicarage at South Bersted in 1465. Before this date, the chapel was in the parish of Pagham until the late 17th century.

The site of the chapel is unknown and at low tides a large group of rocks known as "Bognor Rock" are, said according to legend, to be the remains of the old settlement of Bognor and its Medieval chapel. These rocks are a reef of the Eocene deposits. It is said that the site of the chapel is out at sea opposite Gloucester Road (pictured here). Bognor is Saxon, which goes back to 680 AD when it was known as Buchan-Ora. It was a fishing hamlet.

Boxgrove

The church at Boxgrove dedicated to St Mary and St Blaise was originally the monastic church of Boxgrove priory. It became the parish church when the priory was dissolved in 1536 and the parish church fell into decay. The Benedictine priory was built in the 12th century on the site of a Saxon church, which was mentioned in the Domesday Book. This Saxon building was probably a Collegiate church.

The parish church and priory consisted of a nave, chancel, central tower, north and south aisles, chapter house, cloister, guesthouse and other buildings. Some of the monastic buildings are visible today as ruins north of the church. In the church are a 15th century octagonal font, painted ceiling, and a chantry chapel called the de la Warr chantry built in 1532. The south porch was once a 14th century chapel and became a porch when the priory church became the parish church.

The original parish church, which was to the west of the tower, consisted of a nave, north and south aisles. Only a small section of the nave exists today. The remaining parts of the old church are the south wall, which exists as raised ground and walling. Arcading between the aisles still exists and those to the north aisle are blocked. Masonry of the north wall of the nave still stands at the west end.

Bramber Bridge Chapel

A stone bridge was built in Bramber in 1190, replacing an earlier wooden one. It was between 170 and 200 feet in length, but only 17 feet wide. The centre was 62 x 24 feet and designed to carry a chapel. The bridge chapel dedicated to St Mary was probably built in 1283, although not mentioned until 1304. The chapel would have been rather small with an archway for traffic to go through.

This bridge chapel may not have received much in the way of offerings and in 1412 had very few possessions. A monk was cleared with omitting divine service in 1437 and by 1459 the bridge and chapel were in need of repair. An indulgence was granted in 1468 to contribute to repair the bridge, but by the latter part of the 15th century it fell into decay.

In the 16th century banks were built to prevent flooding and covered most of the bridge and chapel. Piers of the bridge exist today below ground level, but there are no remains of the chapel to be seen. Its name exists today in St Mary's House, which is a 15th century timber-framed building. The site of the old bridge and chapel is along The Street to the east of the house.

Broomhill

The village of Broomhill was deserted due to coastal erosion and silting over a few centuries with the main damage occurring in the great storms of 1287. The church was built at the start of the 13th century and the last services ceased in the 16th century when inroads from the sea ruined it. It is marked as a ruin on some 16th century maps.

The site of the church is shown on old maps and excavations in the 1980s recovered its plan. Substantial flooding in the area from the 13th century was found, indicated by silt on the church floor. There is a slight mound and a scatter of stones in a field east of some works marking the site of the church today.

Bulverhythe

Bulverhythe was once a town, port and harbour, which was mainly lost to sea by coastal erosion in the 17th century. It was one of the limbs of the Cinque port town of Hastings and the only remains of Bulverhythe today are the Bull Inn and ruins of the church. Bulverhythe and its church were not mentioned in the Domesday Book and was known as Bulewar and Buleworehethe in the 12th century.

The church dedicated to St Mary dates from the 14th century and was the second or possibly the third on the site. There are Norman and early English materials in the stonework of the existing church ruins and on the north side of the nave is a section of a Norman arch, 13th century moulding and other designs, which show that the church was built and rebuilt.

The 14th century church consisted of a tower, nave and chancel. It was probably in ruins since the original port was lost. The eastern part of the church still stands in ruins and a road was built over the site of the tower. Excavations at the site found a human skull and remains of a skeleton of the Medieval period. The area around the church is now built over.

Charlton

The village of Charlton west of Bognor was a Saxon tithing of Pagham and mentioned in a pre-Conquest charter as "Ceorla tun". It was lost to the sea by coastal erosion in the 16th century including 16 acres of land. A road in Pagham called "Sea Lane" going in a south-easterly direction and another in Aldwick "Barrack Lane" going south-westerly led to Charlton and converge about 800 yards from the present shore line.

A piece of land called "Churchcroft" may have got its name from the site of a church or chapel, which existed in Medieval times. However there is no suggestion that Charlton ever had a church and, if it did, it would also be in the sea. It is possible that this church became lost sometime before inroads of the sea, and that only its site lies beneath the waves. There are no visible remains to be seen of Charlton or its church at low tide.

Chichester All Saints in the Pallant

In Medieval times there were twelve churches in Chichester. Eight of these were within the walls and were St Peter the Less, St Olaves, St Andrew Oxmarket, St Martin and St Peter sub Castro, All Saints in the Pallant, St Andrew in the Pallant and St Mary-in-Foro (in the market). Also within the walls were two chapels of St Faith and St Cyriac. None of these churches are now in use as a place of worship as they are either gone or in use for other functions. The other two churches outside the walls are still in use and are St Bartholomews and St Pancras.

The church of All Saints in the Pallant in the south-east quadrant of Chichester dates from the 13th century. The Domesday Book of 1086 records in the Archbishop of Canterbury's Hundred of Pagham, a church in Chichester and a rent of 64 pence. This church is thought to be All Saints, in which case the 13th century building stands on the site of a Saxon one.

The present church has no division between nave and chancel and is built of flint and stone with the north wall covered with rough-cast. The 13th century south door is blocked and there is a 15th century door on the west wall. It has a bell turret, lancets and a 19th century north vestry. The church closed for worship after World War II and is now the headquarters for the local branch of the Red Cross.

Chichester St Andrew Oxmarket

This church, in the north-east quadrant of Chichester, was built in the 13th century. At this time the city was a flourishing market town and the name Oxmarket came from the cattle market in East Street, which was closed when the new market was opened at Eastgate in 1872.

The church is complete and like that of All Saints in the Pallant has no division between nave and chancel. It has a bellcote with short spire, west doorway, lancets at the east end of the south and north walls, and 14th and 15th century windows. There are traces of a blocked south doorway. In the grounds, gravestones are used as paving stones.

The church was damaged by a bomb in World War II and after this it ceased to be used as a place of worship. The building is now in use as an arts centre, which opened in 1975. When the centre extended on the north side human bones were found, which were in the old churchyard, and were re-interred in the courtyard in 1988 and marked by a plaque. Also found during the building of a road was a crypt which belongs to the church.

Chichester St Martin

The church of St Martin, which stood in the north-east quadrant, was also known as St Martin in the Pig Market or St Martin in Hoggelane. It stood on the north-eastern corner of St Martin's Square. It was built in the 13th century and consisted of a nave, chancel, north aisle and bell tower with a spire. There were two bells. The nave of the church was in need of repair in the 15th century.

The church was in a bad state of repair at the beginning of the 19th century and was pulled down in 1906. During its demolition a late 13th century mural painting was found. Today the site is a walled garden called St Martin's. The north wall of this garden is part of the old church where there is a blocked window.

Chichester St Olave's

The church dedicated to St Olave dates from Saxon times and is the oldest building in Chichester. It is in the north-east quadrant and its foundation was sometime between 1030 and 1066. It consists of a nave, 13th century chancel, which is at an angle to the north-east and a bellcote with a short spire. The west door is of the 14th century and the floor of the chancel is paved with tiles of the 15th and 17th centuries.

The church was restored in 1850/51 and a circular arch to an undercroft under the chancel came to light. The south door of the nave is the main surviving Saxon feature of the church. There is a 13th century piscina on the north wall of the nave and a mural in the south wall of the chancel came from St Martin's church.

St Olave's church was closed for worship in the 1950s and is now in use as a SPCK bookshop. SPCK have been publishers and booksellers for nearly 300 years. The church is still consecrated and only one service is held once a year in it on St Olave's Day on July 29.

Chichester St Peter the Less

The church dedicated to St Peter the Less stood on the east side of North Street in the north-east quadrant. It consisted of a tower, nave, chancel and south aisle. The nave could be Saxon, but most of the building dates to the 13th century with the tower and south aisle being added in the 14th century. The church was built of flint and rubble with stone dressings. The tower had two flint and stone buttresses.

The church underwent restorations in 1861/62 and the chancel was centrally aligned with the nave. There were several 18th and 19th century monuments inside the building. The church was also known as St Peter the Great, St Peter by the Guildhall, St Peter la Grande by the Guildhall and St Peter in North Street before the Reformation. The church was demolished in 1957 and shops now occupy the site.

Church Norton

The chapel at Church Norton dedicated to St Wilfrid is only the chancel of the original parish church of Selsey of which the nave was taken down and moved to its present site in 1866. The original church was dedicated to St Peter and consisted of a nave, chancel and bellcote. The new church some one and a half miles to the south, was built in 1866, also dedicated to St Peter and material from the old nave was used to build it, including the Norman pillars.

St Wilfrid's chapel dates from the 13th century and probably stands on the site of a Saxon church. The chapel contains a tomb of John Lewis and his wife Agnes who died in 1537. This area was the original Selsey and in 681 a cathedral was built by St Wilfrid nearby dedicated to St Peter. It had 25 bishops between 681 and 1075. The cathedral is now under the sea due to coastal erosion and no remains of it can be seen at low tide. They say that the bells can still be heard on stormy nights.

Cudlow

Cudlow and its church are now under the sea, like that of nearby Atherington. Cudlow was a port and a sizeable village in 1540 when Littlehampton was only a hamlet. At the end of the 16th century the village was drowned by the waves and the church was almost a ruin. The church still stood until it finally fell victim to the encroaching sea. Thomas Hall was the last rector in 1546.

Today only a few rocks are visible at low tide although residents claim that foundations can be seen at low spring tides. On visiting the area at one very low tide the author noticed rocks which looked like the foundations of a building. Could these be the remains of the old church?

In September 1961 three teenagers found part of a tombstone and a wall when trying to locate the site of the village. They also discovered six blocks of masonry covering an area of ten by ten yards. These appear to be of Caen stone which is used in church building. They were unable to bring these rocks to the surface and they are probably still under the sea to this day.

Duncton

The old church dedicated to St Mary at Duncton was pulled down in 1876 and consisted of a single room with a bellcote. On the site today is a dip where the church stood and only graves remain standing in the churchyard all overgrown with trees. A church at Duncton was mentioned in the Domesday Book.

The new church at Duncton dedicated to the Holy Trinity has the second oldest dated bell (1369) in England. It is inscribed DE FLOTE AÖE LA: HAGUE: FET: LAN: MCCCLXIX. This was probably a navigational bell, which was captured in 1377 by raiders in a Normandy port. This bell was in the old church. Also from the old church is a communion plate including a cup dated 1568.

Exceat

A stone today marks the site of the church at Exceat about two and a half miles east of Seaford. It was early Norman in date and was in ruins by 1640 after the village it served was lost by the plague. The foundations of the church were seen marked in the grassland known as "Chapel Field" in the dry summer of 1913. Excavations were carried out in 1913 and some interesting items were found.

Of the finds were fragments of 15th century stained glass, moulded stones and several skeletons covered with a Purbeck marble slab close to the arch of the church. The church had an interesting apsidal chancel in the shape of a horseshoe and it is said that no other church has one like it, apart from modern ones. There may have been a north porch at one time, but this is not certain. Foundations of the church are discernible on the site around the stone.

Ḣastings Collegiate Churcḣ

The collegiate church dedicated to St Mary-in-the-Castle stands in the grounds of Hastings castle, but not part of it. There may have been a small church on this site going back to Saxon times. It was rebuilt and enlarged as a collegiate church by Robert d'Eu in 1070. The church was incorporated into the castle sometime later.

The church was cruciform in shape and consisted of a nave, chancel, central tower, south aisle, chapter house and south transept. The latter was the chapel of the Holy Cross. In the 12th and 13th centuries the church had twelve Canons and a Dean. Services were the main role, but the Canons trained priests in it, had a school for boys, and choral singing was taught as well.

The church was still in use after the castle became a ruin, but it was dissolved by Henry VIII in 1546. The remains of the church still standing are the central tower, chancel arch, chapter house on the north side of chancel, the walls of the chapel of the Holy Cross and the south aisle. There are some graves in the latter.

Ḣastings Parish Churches

Apart from the collegiate church in the castle, Hastings had a total of seven churches in Medieval times. They were All Saints, St Andrew, St Clement, St Leonard, St Margaret, St Michael and St Peter. These were all mentioned in 1291 and by 1372 only All Saints, St Andrew, St Clement and St Leonard were mentioned. Today only All Saints and St Clement are standing and in use.

All the other churches were either lost to the sea by coastal erosion or destroyed by French attacks between the 14th and 15th centuries. In 1834 the foundations of St Michael's church were identified when the coastguard station was built and fragments of a building was found at the south-west edge of the east cliff, which are said to be the remains of St Peter's church (possible site pictured here).

The original St Clement's church fell victim to the sea in the 13th century and a new one was erected further inland in 1286. This was destroyed by French raids in 1378 and a new church was built in 1380. There are no visible remains of these lost churches to be seen today including those lost to the sea by coastal erosion.

Ḟastings St Leonard's

The parish church dedicated to St Leonard was the westernmost of the Hastings churches. It was a Norman building founded by one of the Eu family and could have been built on the site of a Saxon church. It consisted of a nave and chancel. The Black Death and inroads by the sea affected the parish in the mid-14th century.

Damaged by the French in the war of 1377, the church became a free chapel in 1458, and survived after the parish was depopulated. By 1548 the inhabitants went to the church at nearby Hollington. St Leonard's church stood at the top of a cliff as a ruin by the beginning of the 19th century. St Leonard's was built as a new town in 1828 and a new parish church was constructed in 1831.

The site of the original St Leonard's church is uncertain, but stood at the top of Norman Road possibly near the junction of Mercatoria on the south side. This area is now occupied by the Mercatoria Business Centre. The modern Methodist church in Norman Road probably occupies the site of the old churchyard.

Heene

There has been a church at Heene since Saxon times and it is likely that one of the two churches mentioned in the Domesday Book at Terringes (West Tarring) may have been the one at Heene. It is doubtful whether the Saxon church stood on the site of the 13th century one. It may have been further to the south and lost to the sea by coastal erosion.

The 13th century building was abandoned about the turn of the 18th century and consisted of a nave, chancel and steeple. No baptisms or burials ever took place in the chapel. Today only the east end of the chancel survives as a ruin in the grounds of the modern church of St Botolph, Heene, which was built in 1873. There is a 14th century font in the ruin.

Iham

The parish church of Iham near Winchelsea dedicated to St Leonard dates from the Saxon period. It was abandoned by the turn of the 16th century. The ruins were still standing in 1763 and probably removed in 1810 when Iham windmill was built on the site. This windmill was restored in 1980 and devastated by the great hurricane of 1987. On the site today is a mound where the church once stood and the existing ruins of the windmill.

It is possible that one of the five churches mentioned in the Domesday Book under Rameslie may have been at Iham. According to W D Cooper's history of Winchelsea c.1850 it states that the five churches were at Rye (St Mary), two in Winchelsea (St Thomas and St Giles), one in Brede (St George) and the other at St Leonards near Winchelsea, which is at Iham despite being described as the "part of the town and port of Hastings".

Islesham

The village of Islesham and its Medieval chapel some one and a half miles west of Littlehampton was once believed to have been lost to the sea by coastal erosion in the Middle Ages. It is now thought to be more inland in the vicinity of Kent's Farm to the south of Climping. Islesham was north-east of Bailiffscourt on John Speed's map of 1610 and John Blaue's map of 1645.

The site of the chapel is not certain and there are a few possibilities for its location. One of these sites being east of Kent's Farm, another some way south of it, and the third site being where Climping St Mary School now stands. The author believes its site may be in a field north of Kent's Farm as there appears to be a rectangular hump (site pictured here) facing east to west.

A footpath called Bread Lane, which goes to the sea from the school was named from a field called "Holybreadths". This field was south of the school and is probably land which was charged with the payment for Holy Bread. It is referred to in the rubics at the end of the Communion service of the 1549 prayer book. Was the chapel near this field?

Kingston

At one time a village and chapel existed at Kingston, west of Ferring, which was mainly lost to sea by coastal erosion in the 17th century. There is little information about Kingston chapel which was built in the 13th century. It was a rectangular building and its roof was made with Horsham stone. The chapel is marked on Saxton's map of 1575, the Armada map of 1587 and a map of 1669, but not on one dated 1770.

There is a premonition made by Kingston churchwardens in 1626 "Our chappell is much decayed by reason of the sea". Also there is an undated letter written by a Ferring vicar, which reads "The last service has taken place in the chapel as the waves are washing up the sides of the walls which were almost surrounded at high tide". The chapel had disappeared beneath the waves by 1641.

At low tide, a group of rocks known as "Black Rock" can be seen and are said to be the remains of Kingston chapel. It is also said that the bells can still be heard ringing at low tide. These rocks are some half a mile out at sea and the chapel was half this distance, but could have been washed further out when it fell victim to the waves.

Lewes All Saints

In Medieval times Lewes had 14 parish churches. Ten of these were inside the Medieval walls of the town and four outside. Only six remain standing today and only five are in use as a place of worship, which are St Anne, St John the Baptist, Southover, St John-sub-Castro (under the castle), St Michael and St Thomas at Cliffe. Most of these churches underwent restorations in the 19th century, particularly that of St John-sub-Castro.

All that remains of the Medieval church of All Saints is the flint tower, which has diagonal buttresses on the west. The 14th or 15th century nave, chancel and north transept chapel were pulled down in 1806 and replaced by a brick nave with two tier windows. The stone chancel and transepts were built in 1883. All Saints is now in use as a youth and arts centre with a stage and seating.

At the eastern end of the churchyard is a 15th century archway which is said to have come from the Grey Friars. The monuments inside All Saints' church suffered some damage during restoration. Two of these are of Robert Hasford who died in 1624 and John Stansfield who died in 1627. There are also some 18th century monuments on the walls.

Lewes St Nicholas-in-Foro

The church of St Nicholas-in-Foro stood at the top of School Hill. It was left to ruin sometime in the 15th century. The tower survived and was known as "The broken church". A bell called "Gabriel" cast in 1555 was hung in the tower to ring the curfew and in 1690 Thomas Garrat was paid four pounds yearly for ringing the bell at four in the morning and eight at night.

The remains of St Nicholas-in-Foro church were demolished in 1761 and the bell was hung in the Market Tower, which was built in 1792, where it still is today. On the site of the church today stands the war memorial at the junction of the High Street and Market Street. When a new water main was being laid in 1934 two skeletons were found near the site of the church. St Nicholas-in-Foro had no churchyard and the bodies were probably buried inside the church.

Lewes St Peter Westout

The church dedicated to St Peter Westout (outside the westgate) stood just outside the westgate of the walled town and was demolished in 1536/38. The parish was merged with that of St Anne in 1583. The site of St Peter Westout is now Trevor House, which was built from stones from the old church. It was the vicarage until the 1950s and is now a private residence. Bits of masonry from the church are embedded in a wall in Rotten Row.

The other lost churches in Lewes are Holy Trinity, St Andrew, St Martin, St Mary-in-Foro, St Peter the Less and St Sepulchre. None of these are visible above ground, but some survive in street names off the High Street where they once stood such as St Martins Lane and St Andrews Lane. Some of these were only small churches which served their parishes.

Linch

The parish of Linch or Lynch consisted of two parts in Medieval times. A southern part near Bepton, which had a church, and a northern part six miles away at Woodmansgreen where there is a chapel. The main settlement was the southern part where a village once existed, which was deserted due to the Black Death in the Middle Ages.

The parish church at Linch was mentioned in the Domesday Book and probably abandoned in the late 15th century. It may have been dedicated to St Luke. The church stood in the stackyard of Linch Farm west of the farmhouse (now demolished) and no trace of it is visible above ground today. In the 18th and 19th centuries a vast quantity of human bones and a Medieval stone coffin were found on the site.

The chapel at the northern end of the parish at Woodmansgreen was built in about 1520 and dedicated to St Luke. This chapel became a ruin in the 17th century and is marked on John Speed's map of 1610 as "St Luke's chapel". It was rebuilt in 1700 and consists of a nave, chancel, south porch and small spire.

Lullington

Lullington, near Alfriston, has a very small church, which is only 16 feet square. It is claimed to be the smallest church in England, but is in fact only the chancel of the original church. This also applies to other churches which claim to be the smallest. The smallest complete church in England is at Calbone, in Somerset, which has a nave, chancel and steeple.

The first church at Lullington dates from 1180 and consisted of a tower, nave and chancel. The second church, which dates from c.1350, had a nave, chancel and porch. The third church dating from the 16th century also had a nave, chancel and porch, re-using material from the 14th century building. The nave of the third church was in ruins when it was burnt down by Oliver Cromwell in the 17th century.

The existing chancel, which was also partly ruined had a west wall built in 1806 for services to commence, so it is not completely lost. Excavations were carried out at the church from April 1965 to July 1966 and on completion the site was returfed. During excavations roofing tiles, graves, glass, pottery and other items were found. Fragments of the nave can still be seen on the site today.

Middleton

The church of St Nicholas, Middleton, was lost to sea by coastal erosion. The church consisted of a tower, nave, chancel, south aisle and porch. It was a 13th century building built on the foundations of a Saxon one, which was mentioned in the Domesday Book. It stood on the west side of Sea Lane, which leads out to the sea.

In 1724 the south aisle of the church was only 60 feet from the high tide mark and by the end of the 18th century the tower and most of the chancel had fallen. In 1795 the church was on the very edge of a low cliff and by 1837 it fell victim to the encroaching sea. It is said that the ruins of the church can be seen at low tide and that the bells can still be heard chiming on stormy nights. At low tide just a few rocks are visible and one looks like a pillar which may have come from the church. Also farmhouses, cottages and five inns were lost to the sea.

Further inland a new church also dedicated to St Nicholas was built at Middleton in 1849. It consists of a nave, apsidal chancel, porch and bellcote. A register dating from 1560 and an Elizabethan chalice and paten dated 1576 are in the new church which came from the old one. In the churchyard are some 18th century tombstones, which were washed up on the beach and came from the old church. One of them is dated 1775.

Milland

Milland chapel, dedicated to St Luke, was built as a chapel of ease to Trotton sometime in the 16th century, probably on the site of a 12th century church or even one going back to Saxon times. The Saxon church was probably a wooden building. The chapel consisted of a nave and chancel under one roof. In the 19th century a transept, porch and a store were added on the north side. There is also a bellcote and two piscinas in the south wall.

In the early part of the 20th century the chapel was used as a Sunday school and then it became out of use. The modern church, also dedicated to St Luke, was built in 1878 in the grounds of the old chapel. It contains an ancient font which probably came from the original Saxon church. Milland chapel is also known as Tuxlith chapel. It is some way from Milland village which is a modern place and perhaps a settlement once existed near the original church.

Northeye

The town of Northeye north-west of Bexhill was an important sea port, which was probably lost during the great storms of the 13th century and was submerged. Its site is known today as "Town Field" and its first chapel stood on the heights of Hill Farm. Two churches were mentioned in the Domesday Book for Bexhill and it is possible that one of them was that at Northeye. This means that a church existed here in Saxon times.

When the land was reclaimed from the sea in the 14th century a new town and chapel was built at Northeye about half a mile south of the old one. This new town was deserted in the 15th century and the chapel built by William de Northeye may have continued to be used until the 16th century.

The ruins of the chapel were marked on 17th and 18th century maps and existed until the 19th century. The size and shape of the chapel could be defined during the hot summer of 1859. It consisted of a small tower, nave and chancel as far as its foundations have been traced. The site of the chapel is now called "Chapel Field" where there is a mound.

Nyetimber

Nyetimber is a small hamlet, about a mile east of Pagham, which has an Inn and a cluster of cottages one of which was a forge. The chapel was part of Barton Manor and is now in use as a dining room for a rest home. Before conversion the north, south and east walls of the chapel were fairly complete and there was only part of the west wall. The chapel was built in about 1220 and is of a later date than the manor. It was used as both a manorial and hamlet chapel.

Old Erringham

The chapel of Old Erringham, some two miles north of Shoreham, is only the chancel of a larger building. The chapel probably dates from the 11th or 12th century and may have fallen into ruin after the desertion of the village in the 14th century which it served. The chapel originally consisted of a nave and chancel. The foundations of the nave are traceable in dry weather and were excavated in 1957 when many items were found such as pottery, brick, tile and graves. Also found were some Post Medieval post holes.

The remaining part of the chapel, known as "The Chapel", has a two light window with mullion on the east wall of the Transitional period which is partly blocked. There are two small openings on the north and south walls which are Norman. The chapel has a modern corrugated tin roof and a concrete floor which was in use as a storage shed for the nearby farm. It is in a front garden on private farmland.

Ore

The parish church at Ore, near Hastings, dedicated to St Helen, was built in the Saxon or early Norman period. The tower was added in the late 12th or 13th century. A south aisle was added in the 18th century. The church was altered during the Medieval period. In the north wall of the nave is a small window, only nine inches, which gives a date to the mid-twelfth century or earlier.

In 1868 it was decided that the church was in too bad a state to be repaired and was abandoned. Today the church stands in ruins and the tower, part of the nave and north and east part of the chancel still remain. A new church, also dedicated to St Helen, was built at Ore in 1869 and contains a late 14th century brass of an unknown couple. This was preserved from the old church.

Pagham St Andrew's Chapel

The present church at Pagham, which is dedicated to St Thomas à Becket, dates from Norman times, but was built on the site of an earlier Saxon church. Further to the west, near the vicarage in the garden of Little Welbourne, are the remains of St Andrew's chapel next to Pagham Harbour.

This chapel, which is mentioned in Caedualla's charter as "The church of St Andrew as on the east bank of the harbour" was called "Uedring Mutha". It may once have been the parish church of Wythering, which was a borough port and township in the vicinity of Pagham, and it declined in the 15th century. There is no sign of Wythering to be seen today.

The remaining part of the chapel consists of a wall between nave and chancel built of rubble. The chancel arch of the 13th century and other windows are blocked up and there are no visible remains to show the original extent of nave and chancel of the chapel. It may have once had a tower, which probably fell into the adjacent harbour to the west.

Preston

The present church dedicated to St Peter at Preston, north of Brighton, dates from the 13th century, but one was mentioned here in the Domesday Book. The church consists of a tower, pyramidal cap, chancel and north porch and is virtually unaltered since the Medieval period. There are 14th century wall paintings inside the church which were damaged by a fire in 1906.

Preston church has been disused since 1988 and all services are now held in the church of St John the Evangelist, built in 1908, which is now the parish church of Preston. The old church is open to the public to visit at times and is cared for by the Redundant Churches Fund. It stands next to the Preston manor house, which is also open to the public.

Robertsbridge

The chapel at Robertsbridge dedicated to Our Lady dates from the 13th century although it was not mentioned until about 1314. It consisted of a nave, chancel and belfry. It was located within the street (which surrounded it) at the southern end of the village. There is no mention of this chapel after the mid-16th century and it was probably demolished at this time or early in the 17th century.

The site of the chapel today is occupied by the present High Street at the junction of Piper's Lane just north of the war memorial. This is east of The Green where there are some 15th century cottages which stand on the site of the Cistercian Abbey at Robertsbridge founded in 1176. This abbey was moved to its present site about a mile to the east in 1210 where it stands in ruins today.

Rumboldswyke

The church of St Mary at Rumboldswyke to the south-east of Chichester dates from the 11th century. It consists of a nave, chancel, north aisle, organ chamber and a bell turret. The latter was a bellcote in the 18th century and there is a round arch made of sandstone between the nave and chancel. According to Lower the original dedication of the church was to St Rumbold.

The walls of the church are made with knapped flints and some herringbone masonry of Roman brick. The church underwent some restoration in 1866 and a north aisle was added. The interior was plastered white. The church became out of use in the 1980s and is now offices. It stands in a built-up area and is a suburb of Chichester locally called Whyke.

St Roche's Chapel

St Roche's chapel stood within the Iron Age hillfort on St Roche's Hill (known today as "The Trundle") to the south of Singleton. St Roche's Hill was known as St Roch, St Rock's, St Rokeshill or St Rooks over the centuries. St Roche was a French saint who was born in the early 14th century and died in the mid-14th century. No chapel in his honour was probably built until the latter part of the 14th century.

St Roche's chapel was built sometime between 1375 and 1400 and was probably abandoned at the Reformation. There is very little information about the chapel but it was a rectangular building 14 by 11 feet. It was described as "Late chappell of St Rooks" in 1570 and was still standing in ruins by 1723. Today the site is represented by a mound. Brick, stone and tile, of which the chapel was constructed, can still be found on the site.

South Heighton

The parish church of South Heighton dedicated to St Martin dates from the Medieval period. It was struck by lightning and gutted by fire in 1769 and the few parishioners were too poor to repair the church. In the 18th century only one wall remained plus several graves. The ruins were marked on an 1879 map and the basin of the font is now in Chiddingly church.

The interior of South Heighton church and its cemetery were used as a garden until a house called 'The Hall' was built on the site in the latter part of the 19th century. This hall was pulled down in the year 2000 and now two houses occupy the site. Garden walls of the hall still stand on the site today and human bodies were moved from here to another cemetery.

Sutton

The parish church of Sutton near Seaford dates from the 12th century. It consisted of a nave, chancel, aisles and possibly a tower. Notable defects were found in the chancel in the 15th century, and the church became desolate and roofless in the 16th century. The village which it served was deserted in the late 14th or early 15th century.

The remains of the church were still visible in the 19th century and in 1858 it was reported that "The church has long been destroyed though its foundations are clearly traceable". It stood in the grounds of Sutton Place (a 16th century house now in use as a school) and the grounds were re-turfed in 1949.

Due to the dry summer of 1949 and spring 1950 the outline of the church was discernible in the turf. It measured 90 feet in length and 40 feet in width and a square projection was seen at the west end which was probably a tower. Human remains of the 12th century were found, one of which being a child. The area north of Sutton Place is now built over and the site of the church (pictured here) stood east of Sandore Close just south of a wall.

Treyford

The old church of Treyford, dedicated to St Mary, dates from the 13th century. It was closed for worship in the mid-19th century and was left to decay and has been in ruins since. It was an un-aisled building consisting of a nave and chancel and had a north porch. The church once had a 14th century north chapel. Only the east, west and south walls of the church remain which are very overgrown together with the graveyard. The church is situated on a small hill near Treyford Farm.

In 1849 a new church was built at Treyford which consisted of a tower, spire, nave and chancel. It was known as "The cathedral of the Downs" due to its large size in so small a village. This church served the villages of Treyford and Elsted. The Saxon church at Elsted was damaged by a falling tree in 1889 and was rebuilt in 1952. In 1951 the new Treyford church was blown up due to crumbling walls and sinking foundations, but its churchyard is still used for burials. Today Treyford has two churchyards but no church.

West Marden

There are four Mardens, East, West, North and Up. All have churches apart from that of West Marden, but it did possess one in Medieval times and no sign of it exists above ground today. It was mentioned in 1414 and 1525 and it is thought that it ceased to be used for worship sometime before 1585. The church probably fell into ruins by the 17th century. West Marden is the biggest of the four villages.

In Up Marden church, which dates from the 13th century on the site of a Saxon one, is a triangular chancel arch which is Saxon. This was a 16th century addition to the church to support the 13th century arch. It is said that the stones of the triangular arch came from the former church at West Marden when it was no longer in use. This means that West Marden church dates from the Saxon period.

Winchelsea

The old town of Winchelsea was lost to the sea after great storms in the 13th century. This town had a harbour, some 300 houses, 50 inns, a Greyfriars and two churches dedicated to St Thomas and St Giles (two of the five churches mentioned in the Domesday Book under Rameslie). In the same century a new town for Winchelsea was built on Iham Hill, but this declined in size in Medieval times. This new town also had two churches dedicated to St Thomas and St Giles.

Of the churches in the new town only St Thomas survives (pictured here), but only the chancel with north and south chapels are in use today. This church was built in the early part of the 14th century, but was mostly destroyed by the French some 60 years later. The nave and aisles no longer exist and the transepts are in ruins. There was once a detached bell tower which was demolished in 1790. There are 13th century monuments in the church.

St Giles church was smaller than that of St Thomas and was built in the 14th century. It probably became defunct in the early part of the 16th century and its ruins remained until 1777. There are no visible remains of the church to be seen today. A lane called Deadmans Lane by the church got its name from the French who sacked the town in 1350. Many people took refuge in St Giles church but they were butchered therein.

Worthing

The Medieval chapel at Worthing was probably built in the 13th century. At this time Worthing was just a small fishing village. The chapel was mentioned in 1291, 1380 and used for mass in 1410. A note from Bishop Rede's Register "Licencia celebrandi in capella de Worthyng" dated February 14, 1409 states "to hear Masses and other Divine offices in the chapel of Worthing upon a portable alter".

The chapel was still in existence in the 16th century and in private hands by 1575. It was demolished in about 1635. Worthing chapel was probably a small single-chambered building built of flint, but it may have been wooden.

The site of the chapel is unknown and was once thought to have been lost to the sea by coastal erosion. It is now thought that the chapel was further inland in the vicinity of The Swan Inn at the northern end of the High Street. There is a green area just south of the pub (pictured here), which could well be the site of the chapel.